Matilda Chaplin Ayrton

Child-life in Japan, and Japanese child-stories

Matilda Chaplin Ayrton

Child-life in Japan, and Japanese child-stories

ISBN/EAN: 9783742830180

Manufactured in Europe, USA, Canada, Australia, Japa

Cover: Foto ©Andreas Hilbeck / pixelio.de

Manufactured and distributed by brebook publishing software (www.brebook.com)

Matilda Chaplin Ayrton

Child-life in Japan, and Japanese child-stories

AND

JAPANESE CHILD-STORIES.

Extracts from some Press Notices of the First Edition.

"A curious work. The illustrations by native artists are very quaint."—*Times.*

"Will greatly interest and instruct both young and old."—*Daily Chronicle.*

"Possesses an abiding interest for readers of all ages. . . . the daily life of a most engaging people."—*Daily News.*

"This book will be as good as a pantomime to children, and something better to their elders."—*Academy.*

"The quaint strange pictures, and life of Japanese children are very interesting."—*Standard.*

"Gives a vivid idea of the nursery lore of this remarkable people."—*Queen.*

"People who want a child's gift book quite out of the ordinary groove can get it by procuring 'Child Life in Japan.'"—*Church Times.*

"A very quaint and beautiful volume. A glimpse of the 'land of the rising sun.'"—*Western Morning News.*

"No more delightful book could be presented to little people."—*Scotsman.*

"Very amusing, and calculated to promote infinite laughter."—*Globe.*

"Decidedly amusing . . . . with quaint Japanese pictures and funny stories."—*Morning Post.*

"A fascinating child's book."—*Spectator.*

"Must fascinate most children by its quaint pictures."—*Examiner.*

"We give this volume our heartiest commendation."—*Glasgow Herald.*

"A genuine novelty in the way of children's books."—*Sporting and Dramatic News.*

"A tempting book. The stories are singularly exciting."—*Art Journal.*

"A veritable and attractive novelty."—*British Quarterly Review.*

"Gives a vivid picture of domestic life in Japan."—*Liverpool Albion.*

KANGURA. Front.

CHILD-LIFE IN JAPAN,

AND

JAPANESE CHILD-STORIES.

BY

M. CHAPLIN AYRTON,

*Bachelier-ès-Lettres, et Bachelier-ès-Sciences (rest.), Paris,
Civis Academiæ Edinensis,
et
Élève de la Faculté de Médecine de Paris.*

WITH MANY ILLUSTRATIONS, INCLUDING SEVEN FULL-PAGE PICTURES
DRAWN AND ENGRAVED BY JAPANESE ARTISTS.

New and Cheaper Edition.

GRIFFITH, FARRAN, OKEDEN & WELSH,
SUCCESSORS TO NEWBERY AND HARRIS,
WEST CORNER ST. PAUL'S CHURCHYARD, LONDON,
AND SYDNEY, N.S.W.

DEDICATION.

TO ŌJŌSAMA.

"AWAI ko ni mo tabi wo sassero (send the child you love on a journey), as saith great Nipon's proverb,—and whither do *you* soon journey, beloved?" says, showing her black-stained teeth and rubbing the head of the young child she tends, an old Japanese nurse. "To my honoured grandmother of my noble country," lisps the little ladyship whose features, though, neither whose dress nor talk, show her to be a European.

"And what shall I, your grandame here, do when you forsake and forget her?"

"She will weep greatly for her Ōjōsama," and at this sad thought a little dimpled hand caresses consolingly the brown much-loved cheek.

"This kindly folk, this sunny country,—its tea-gardens, its temples, its pine-groves, its rice-fields, even its toys,—all these on which alone her wondering baby-stare has ever hung, all these will be forgotten," a listener says, "for as the lotus in the moat yonder casts its rosy petals, so will these early memories fade; but as nourishing mud to the edible lotus-root so will your love and that of your gentle nation have caused the very roots of this young life to germinate a loving nature that will itself endure and nourish love in others."

INTRODUCTION.

IN almost every English home are Japanese fans, in our shops Japanese dolls and balls and other nicknacks, on our writing-tables bronze crabs or lacquered pen-tray with outlined on it the extinct volcano that is the most striking mountain seen from the capital of Japan; and at European places of amusement Japanese houses of real size have been exhibited, and the jargon of fashion for "Japanese Art" even reaches our children's ears.

Yet all these things seem dull and lifeless when thus severed from the quaint cheeriness of their true home. To those familiar with

Japan, that bamboo fan-handle recalls its graceful grassy tree, the thousand and one daily purposes for which bamboo wood serves, —the open shop where squat the brown-faced artisans cleverly dividing into those slender divisions the fan-handle,—the wood-block engraver's where some dozen men sit patiently chipping at their cherry-wood blocks,—the printer's where the colouring arrangements seem so simple to those used to Western machinery, but where the colours are so rich and true. We see the picture stuck on the fan frame with starch paste, and drying in the brilliant summer sunlight; and the designs recall vividly the life around, whether that life be the stage, the home, insects, birds, or flowers. We think of halts at wayside inns when bowing tea-house girls at once proffer these fans to hot and tired guests.

The tonsured oblique-eyed doll suggests the festival of similarly oblique-eyed little girls on the 3rd of March, when dolls of every degree obtain for a day " Dolls' Rights ;" for in every Japanese household all the dolls of the present and previous generations are on that festival set out to best advantage, with, beside them, sweets, green speckled rice-cake, and daintily gilt and lacquered dolls' utensils. For some time previous, to meet the increased demand, the doll shopman has been very busy, sitting before a straw-holder into which he can readily stick, to dry, the wooden supports of the plaster dolls' heads he is painting, as he takes first one and then another to give artistic touches to their glowing cheeks or little tongue. That dolly that seems but "so odd" to Polly or Maggie is there the cherished darling of its little owner, passing half its day tied on to her back, peeping companionably its head over her shoulder, whilst at night it is lovingly sheltered under the green mosquito curtains and provided with a toy wooden pillow.

The expression "Japanese Art" seems but a created word expressing either the imitations of it or the artificial transplanting of Japanese things to a European house, for the whole glory of art in Japan, is, that it is not *Art*, but *Nature* simply rendered, by a people with a fancy and love of fun quite Irish in character. Just as Greek sculptures were good because in those days artists modelled the corsetless life around them, so the Japanese artist does not draw well his lightly-draped figures, cranes, and insects because these things strike him as beautiful, but because he is familiar with their every action.

The Japanese house brought to Europe seems but a dull and listless affair, we miss the idle, easy-going life and chatter, the tea, the sweetmeats, the pipes and charcoal brazier, the clogs awaiting their wearers on the large flat stone at the entry, the grotesquely-trained ferns, the glass balls and ornaments tinkling in the breeze, that hang, as well as lanterns, from the eaves, the garden with tiny pond and goldfish, bridge and miniature hill, the bright sunshine beyond the sharp shadow of the upward curving angles of the tiled roof, the gay scarlet folds of the women's under-dress peeping out, their little litter of embroidery or mending, and the babies, brown and half naked, scrambling about so happily; for what has a baby to be miserable about in a land where it is scarcely ever slapped, where its clothing, always loose, is yet warm in winter, where it basks freely in air and sunshine, and lives in a house, that from its thick grass mats, its absence of furniture, and therefore of commands "not to touch," is the very beau-ideal of an infant's playground.

The object with which the following pages were written, was that young folks who in England see and handle so often Japanese objects, but who find books of travels thither too long and dull for their reading, might catch a glimpse of the spirit that pervades life in the " Land of the rising Sun." A portion of the book is derived from translations from Japanese tales, kindly given to the author by Mr. Basil H. Chamberlain, whilst the rest was written at idle moments during graver studies.

M. CHAPLIN AYRTON,
École de Médecine, Paris.

CONTENTS.

	PAGE
SEVEN SCENES OF CHILD-LIFE IN JAPAN	2
THE SCRAP-BOOK	15
O'SHOGWATS (NEW YEAR)	23
THE CHRYSANTHEMUM SHOW	41
THE BABES ON THE SEA	49
FISHSAVE	55
THE FILIAL GIRL OF ECHIGO	61
THE PARSLEY QUEEN	65
A WRESTLER AND A SNAKE	69
A FIRE-CARRIAGE FROM HELL	75
THE TWO DAUGHTERS OF OKADA	79
URANAI (SECOND-SIGHT)	87
GAMES	93
APPENDIX—THE GAMES AND SPORTS OF JAPANESE CHILDREN	101

LIST OF FULL-PAGE ILLUSTRATIONS.

KANGURA . . . . *Frontispiece.*

SNOW-BALLING . . . . *Facing p.* 4

MUSICAL BOYS ,, 6

TOP SPINNING . . . . ,, 8

PLAYING WITH PUPPIES . . . . . . ,, 9

BOY ON STILTS ,, 10

THE TURTLE . . . . . . ,, 12

LIST OF SMALLER PICTURES.

GIRLS PLAYING BALL	*Title-page.*
LOTUS FLOWERS IN THE CASTLE MOAT AT YEDO	vii
HOI KANGO, JAPANESE GAME, DESCRIBED ON P. 96.	3
WRESTLING	11
DARUMA, THE SNOW-MAN	13
O'SHU	17
ACROBATS	22
BRONZE FISH FROM A GATEWAY	25
JINGO KOGO	28
THE SEVEN GODS OF WEALTH	33
FIREMEN	39
BOY PLAYING WITH A KANGURA MASK	40
STREET STALL	43
A TOY FESTIVAL CAR	47
THE BABES ON THE SEA DRIFTING AWAY	51
FISHSAVE JOURNEYING TO HIS FATHER	59
THE GIRL OF ECHIGO HONOURING HER MOTHER'S MIRROR.	63
PLAYING AT CARRYING SPIRIT TUBS	67
SANGIASII	81
STORKS	85
NEW YEAR'S DECORATIONS, DESCRIBED ON P. 26	92
BLINDMAN'S BUFF	95
KITE FLYING	99

NOTE.

The device on the cover, representing a red and gold paper string, called MIDZUHIKI, and a paper bag with a piece of seaweed inside, called NOSHI, are the Japanese symbols that the book is a present.

SEVEN SCENES OF CHILD-LIFE
IN JAPAN.

SEVEN SCENES OF CHILD-LIFE IN JAPAN.

THESE little boys all live a long way from England in islands called "Japan." If they invited you to come and see them it would cost two thousand shillings, and take you about fifty-five days to travel in ships and railway trains before you arrived at their home. But as you are too young yet to earn money, and have only enough pennies given you to buy this book and sugar-plums, you must fancy from these pictures what little Jap boys are like. They have all rather brown chubby faces, and they are very merry. Unless they give themselves a really hard knock they seldom get cross or cry.

In the second large picture two of the little boys are playing at snowball. Although it is hotter in the summer in their country than it is in England, the winter is as cold as you feel it; like English boys, these lads enjoy a fall of snow, and still better than snowballing they like making a snow-man with a charcoal ball for each eye and a streak of charcoal for his mouth. The shoes which they usually wear out of doors are better for a snowy day than your boots, for their feet do not sink into the snow, unless it is deep. These shoes are of wood, and make a boy seem to be about three inches taller than he really is. The shoe, you see, has not laces or buttons, but is kept on the foot by that thong which passes between the first and second toe. The thong is made of grass, and covered with strong paper or with white or coloured calico. The boy in the check dress wears his shoes without socks, but you see the

SNOWBALLING.

other boy has socks on. His socks are made of dark blue calico, with a thickly woven sole, and a place, like one finger of a glove, for his big toe. If you were to wear Japanese shoes, you would think the thong between your toes very uncomfortable, but from the habit of wearing this sort of shoe, their big toe grows more separate from the other toes, and the skin between this and the next toe becomes as hard as the skin of a dog's or a cat's paw.

The boys are not cold, for their cotton clothes being wadded, are warm and snug. One boy has a rounded pouch fastened to his sash; it is red, and prettily embroidered with flowers or birds, and is his purse, in which he keeps some little toys and some money. His pence are as big as farthings and halfpennies, but he would want five of his farthings to make up the value of an English farthing. Each piece of money has a square hole in its centre, so that if, for instance, he is a rich little boy possessing perhaps threepence, he puts a bit of straw through these holes and knots it at each end to make all safe, and keep his sixty coins together. The other boy very likely has not a pouch, but he has two famous big pockets, for, like all Japanese, he uses the part of his large sleeve which hangs down as his pocket. Thus when a group of little children are disturbed at play you see each little hand seize a treasured toy and disappear into its sleeve, like mice running into their holes with bits of cheese.

In the next large picture are two boys who are fond of music. One has a flute, which is made of bamboo wood. These flutes are easy to make, as bamboo wood grows hollow with cross divisions at intervals, so that if you cut a piece with a division forming one end you need only make the outside holes in order to finish your flute.

The child sitting down has a drum. His drum and the paper lanterns hanging up have painted on them an ornament which is also the crest of the house of "Arima." If these boys belong to this family they wear the same crest embroidered on the centre of the backs of their coats.

The picture which forms the frontispiece, represents a game called "Kangura," that children in Japan

MUSICAL BOYS.

are very fond of playing at. They are probably trying to act as well as the maskers did whom they saw on New Year's Day, just as English children try and imitate things they see in a pantomime. The masker goes from house to house accompanied by one or two men who play on cymbals, flute, and drum. He steps into a shop where the people of the house and their friends sit drinking tea, and passers-by pause in front of the open shop to see the fun. He takes a mask, like the one in the picture, off his back and puts it over his head. This boar's-head mask is painted scarlet and black, and gilt, and has a green cloth hanging down behind, in order that you may not perceive where the mask ends and the man's body begins. Then the masker imitates an animal. He goes up to a young lady and lays down his ugly head beside her to be patted, as "Beast" may have coaxed "Beauty" in our English fairy tale. He grunts, and rolls, and scratches himself, so that the children almost forget he is a man, and roar with laughter at the funny animal. When they begin to tire of this fun he exchanges this mask for some of the two or three others he carries with him, such as putting on a mask of an old woman over his face, and at the back of his head a very different second mask, a cloth tied over the centre of the head making the two faces yet more distinct from each other. He has quickly arranged the back of his dress to look like the front of a person, and as he acts, first presenting the one person to his spectators, then the other, he makes you even imagine he has four arms, so cleverly can he twist round his arm and gracefully fan what is in reality the back of his head.

The tops the lads are playing with in picture No. 4, are not quite the same shape as our tops, but they spin very well. Some men are so clever at making spinning-tops run along strings, throwing them up into the air and catching them with a tobacco-pipe, that they earn a living by exhibiting their skill.

Some of the tops are formed of short pieces of bamboo with a wooden peg put through them, and the hole cut in the side makes them have a fine hum as the air rushes in whilst they spin.

TOP SPINNING.

PLAYING WITH PUPPIES.

The boys in the next large picture, No. 5, must be playing with the puppies of a large dog, to judge by their big paws. There are a great many large dogs in the streets of Yedo; some are very tame, and will let children comb their hair and ornament them and pull them about. These dogs do not wear collars, as do our pet dogs, but a wooden label bearing the owner's name is hung round their necks. Other big dogs are almost wild.

Half-a-dozen of these dogs will lie in one place, stretched drowsily on the grassy city walls under the trees, during the day-time. Towards evening they rouse themselves and run off to yards and rubbish-heaps to pick up what they can; they will eat fish, but two or three dogs soon get to know where the meat-eating Englishmen live, and come trotting in regularly with a business-like air to search among the day's refuse for bones; should any interloping dog try to establish a right to share the feast he can only gain his footing after a victorious battle. All these dogs are very wolfish-looking, with straight hair, which is usually white or tan-coloured. There are other pet dogs kept in houses;

these look something like spaniels; they are small, with their black noses so much turned up that it seems as if, when they were puppies, they had tumbled down and broken the bridge of the nose. They are often ornamented like dog Toby in "Punch and Judy," with a ruff made of some scarlet stuff round their necks.

After the heavy autumn rains have filled the roads with big puddles, it is great fun, this boy thinks, to walk about on stilts. You see him in plate No. 6. His stilts are of bamboo wood, and he calls them "Sangiash," after the long-legged snowy herons that strut about in the wet rice-fields. When he struts about on them, he wedges the upright between his big and second toe as if the stilt was like his shoes. He has a good view of his two friends who are wrestling, and probably making hideous noises like wild animals as they try to throw one another, for they have seen fat public wrestlers stand on opposite sides of a sanded ring, stoop, rubbing their thighs, and in a crouching attitude and growling, slowly advance upon one another, then when near to one another, the spring is made and the men close. If after some time the round is not

BOYS ON STILTS.

decided by a throw, the umpire, who struts about like a turkey-cock, fanning himself, approaches, and plucks the girdle of the weaker combatant, when the wrestlers at once retire to the side of the arena to rest, and to sprinkle a little water over themselves.

In the neighbourhood in which the children shown in the picture overleaf live, there is a temple, called "Compira," in honour of which a feast-day is held on the tenth of every month, and the tenth day of the tenth month is a yet greater feast-day. On these days they go the first thing in the morning to the barber's to have their heads shaved and dressed, and their faces powdered with white, and their lips and cheeks painted pink. They wear their best clothes and smartest sashes, and then they clatter off on their wooden clogs to the temple and buy two little rice-cakes at the gates. Next they come to two large comical bronze dogs sitting on stands one on each side of the path. They reach up and gently rub the dog's nose, then rub their own noses, rub the dog's eyes, and then their own, and so on till they have touched the dog's and their own body all over. This is their way of praying for good health. They also add another to the number of little rags that have been hung by each visitor about the dog's neck. Then they go to the altar and give their cakes to a boy belonging to the temple, who in exchange presents them with one rice-cake which has been blessed; they ring a round brass bell to call their god's attention, and throw him some money into a grated box as big as a child's crib, and then they squat down and pray to be good little boys. Now they go out and amuse themselves by looking at all the stalls of

THE TURTLE.

toys, and cakes, and flowers, and fish. The man who sells the gold fish, with fan-like tails as long as their bodies, has also turtles, and these boys at last settle that of all the pretty things they have seen they would best like to spend their money on a young turtle. For their pet rabbits and mice died, but turtles, they say, are painted on fans and screens and boxes because turtles live for ten-thousand years, whereas even the noble white crane is said to live no more than a thousand years. In this picture they have carried home the turtle and are much amused at the funny way it walks and peeps its head in and out from under its shell.

THE SCRAP-BOOK.

THE SCRAP-BOOK.

WHO does not know the charm of a scrap-book? I considered myself as a child privileged by the possession of but a third share in one owned with two elder brothers. As a treat there was mother's big scrap-book to pore over, helping us to picture those sweet cloudland days of—"when you were little, mother." Herein were short-waisted damsels, befrilled boys, episodes of coaching days, and political caricatures of "old Bony" and Lord Brougham. My next experience was when seized in maturer years by the ambitious scheme of making a genuine scrap-book, wherein should be gradually accumulated odds and ends, without recourse to those bought sheets of symmetrically arranged pictures that now form in an afternoon the misnamed *scrap*-book. I was assisted by the wise counsel of a pair of youngsters who had opinions so revolutionary as to persist that pigs would look nice next to fairies, and that carts must come before horses, and whose delight it was to dab fat fingers in the paste and then suck them. Separated from these comrades the scrap-book was laid aside unheeded; years passed away; the neglected book was tumbled into a box that was sent to Japan. Here its loose and half-filled leaves were stitched together and the scrap-book re-asserted itself; indeed as I write I look lovingly at its now well-filled and well-thumbed leaves and nice curling corners of pink and blue calico, innocently gaudy and free from modern high art tints and bilious greens, bright with little Parisian lithographs of prettily affected juveniles, here a peacock butterfly, and there a soberer woodcut of romping English children and spreading landscape, and gay withal with brightest of Japanese prints, and of these last is my tale.

An old woman called "the august Grandmother" would set out with the child she loved, pick-a-back, and walk to the neighbouring print-shop. Here arrived, she bowed lowly to the shopman saying a greeting, then seated herself on the raised floor of the shop, loosened with a grunt the string that tied her Ojo-sama (little ladyship) on her back, when the freed child would at once make a dash at the nearest pictures. Most of the pictures are about one foot three by nine inches, and are ranged on strings across the shop-front. Those curious fierce fellows with slanting eyebrows are actors, while amongst other pictures, often in sets of threes, are warriors in lacquered armour, firemen with paper standard and wadded garments, paunchy wrestlers, quaintly-dressed dancers and red-kerchiefed acrobats,—in fact almost every scene or story of Japanese life is pictured; but the literary treacle specially spread to catch the little flies lies upon the shop floor, for there are piles of prints containing smaller prints, often ingeniously arranged, so that, if cut out, a box, or house, or figure can be constructed; coloured paper masks, tiny folding theatres, and little penny picture-books. The child selects her penny book, and this is the tale she chose.

In the olden days, in the province of Shin, there lived with his step-mother a little boy called O'Shu. Now this step-mother was very cruel to poor little O'Shu. If he complained of a pain she, more often than other parents, set light to some leaves of a plant put on O'Shu's back to burn him in many places, and she gave him very little fish to eat, and grudged him even rice; neither would she give him pence to get a bath nor have his hair dressed. But O'Shu was always bright and merry, because he bethought him how his uncle the priest, as they walked in the shady pine-groves of Shiba's lacquered shrines, had told him that Confucius the great and wise had spoken of filial piety as the noblest virtue, and taught him that even unkind parents were to be reverenced by their offspring. Now it happened one day when not only the big mountain Fusi was snow-capped but all the rice-fields were snow-wreathed, when the early white plum-blossoms could only be distinguished from the snow-flakes on the sloping branches by their position on the upright twigs, when scarce dusk the outer shutters were slid forth from their case and closed round the deep-eaved house, when the charcoal braziers were heaped high with glowing embers and friends greeted with "Cold it is truly," "Toast your hands, I pray you,"—that the step-mother of O'Shu exclaimed "Verily, I wish for a dish of fresh fish!" Well, she knew that such a thing as a dish of fresh fish could not be got when all the ponds and rivers were ice-bound. O'Shu, unnoticed, left the room and, slipping on his wooden clogs, his yellow paper rain-coat, and carrying his varnished paper umbrella, he hurried down to the river. Not a single rift could he find in the ice, so the unselfish boy stripped off his clothes and lay himself on the ice to try and melt a hole in it by means of his bodily heat. The heavens were touched by the ignorant lad's filial piety and caused the thick ice to melt, when O'Shu beheld swimming towards him two noble carp, who allowed themselves to be grasped by the shivering but delighted boy. O'Shu then dressed and hurried home, set his fish on a lacquered tray, and, to betoken that they were an offering, he tied round them the red and white paper string called "midzuhiki" and slipped in the folded paper "noshi" containing its quaint symbolic offering of a tiny piece of seaweed. Next O'Shu slid aside the paper screen and was before his parents holding the tray to his forehead, and then, in further token of respect prostrating himself till his forehead touched the soft grass-woven mat, he respectfully presented to his unamiable step-mother the desired delicacy.

O'SHOGWATS.

O'SHOGWATS.

(New Year.)

ITTLE Yoshsan had just finished eating the last of five rice-cakes called "dango," that had been strung on a skewer of bamboo and dipped in Soy sauce, when he said to his little sister, called Chrysanthemum,—"O' Kiku, it is soon the great festival of the New Year." "What shall we do then?" asked little O'Kiku, not clearly remembering the festival of the previous year. Thus questioned, Yoshsan had his desired opening to hold forth on the coming delights, and he replied, "Men will come the evening before the great feast-day and help 'Plumblossom,' our maid, to clean all the house with brush and broom. Others will set up the decoration in front of our honoured gateway; they will dig two small holes and plant a gnarled, black-barked father-pine branch on the left, and the slighter reddish mother-pine branch on the right, they will then put with these the tall knotted stem of a bamboo, with its smooth, hard green leaves that chatter when the wind blows; next they will take a grass rope about as long as a tall man, fringed with grass, and decorated with the 'Gohei,' zigzags of white paper, that our noble father says are meant for rude images of men offering themselves in homage to the august gods."

"Oh, yes! I have not forgotten," interrupts Chrysanthemum, "this cord is stretched from bamboo to bamboo; and 'Plumblossom' says the rope is to bar out the nasty two-toed, red, grey, and black demons, the badgers, the foxes, and other evil spirits from crossing our threshold. But *I* think it is the next part of the arch which is the prettiest, the whole bunch of things they tie in the middle of the rope,—there is the crooked-backed lobster, like a bowed old man, with all around the melia branches, whose young leaves bud before the old leaves fall. There are pretty fern-leaves shooting forth in pairs, and deep down between them the little baby fern-leaf; there is the bitter yellow orange, the 'daidai' whose name, you know, means many parents and children, and a black piece of charcoal, whose name is a pun on our homestead."

"But best of all," says Yoshsan, "*I* like the seaweed 'Hontawara,' for it tells me of our brave Queen Jingo Kogo, who, lest the troops should be discouraged, concealed from the army that her husband the king had died, put on armour, and led the great campaign against Corea.* Her troops, stationed at the margin of the sea, were in danger of defeat on account of the lack of fodder for their horses; when she ordered this hontawara to be plucked from the shore, and the horses, freshened by their meal of seaweed, rushed victoriously to battle. On the bronzed clasp of our worthy father's tobacco-pouch is, our noble father says, Jingo Kogo with her sword and the dear little baby-prince, Hachiman, who was born after the campaign,

* A.D. 200.

and who is now our Warrior God, guiding our troops to victory, and that spirit on whose head squats a dragon has risen partly from the deep, to present an offering to the Queen and the Prince."

"Then there is another seaweed, whose name is a pun on 'rejoicing.' There is the lucky bag that I made, for last year, of a square piece of paper into which we put chestnuts and the roe of a herring and dried persimmon fruit, and then tied up the paper with red and white paper-string, that the sainted gods might know it was an offering."

Yoshsan and his little sister had now reached the great gate ornamented with huge bronze fishes sitting on their throats and twisting aloft their forked tails, that was near their home. So telling his sister she must wait to know more about the great festival till the time arrived, they shuffled off their shoes, bowed, till their foreheads touched the ground, to their parents, ate their evening bowl of rice and saltfish, said a prayer and burnt a stick of incense to many-armed Buddha at the family altar, spread their cotton-wadded quilts, rested their dear little shaved heads, with quaint circlet of hair, on the roll of cotton covered with white paper that formed the cushion of their hard wooden pillows, and fell asleep to their mother's monotonously-chaunted lullaby of "Nen ne ko."

> Sleep, my child, sleep my child,
> Where is thy nurse gone?
> She is gone to the mountains
> To buy thee sweetmeats.
> What shall she buy thee?
> The thundering drum, the bamboo pipe,
> The trundling man, or the paper kite.

The great festival drew still nearer to the children's delight as they watched the previously described graceful bamboo arch rise before their gateposts. Then came a party of three men with an oven, a bottomless tub, and some matting to replace the bottom. They shifted the pole that carried these utensils from their shoulders, and commenced to make the Japanese cake that may be viewed as the equivalent of a Christmas pudding. They mixed a paste of rice and put the sticky mass, to prevent rebounding, on the soft mat in the tub. The third man then beat for a long time the rice cake with a heavy mallet. Yoshsan liked to watch the strong man swing down his mallet with dull resounding thuds. The well-beaten dough was then made up into flattish rounds of varying size on a pastry board one of the men had brought. Three cakes of graduated size formed a pyramid that was placed conspicuously on a lacquered stand, and the cakes were only to be eaten on the 11th of January.

The mother told "Plumblossom" and the children to get their clogs, and overcoats, and hoods, for she was going to get the Daikoku-jimé, and the party shuffled off till they came to a stall where were big grass ropes and fringes and quaint grass boats filled with supposed bales of merchandise in straw coverings, a sun in red paper, and at bow and stern sprigs of fir, the whole brightened by bits of gold leaf, lightly stuck on, that quivered here and there. When the children had chosen the harvest ship that seemed most besprinkled with gold, " Plumblossom " bargained about the price, and the mother, who, as a matter of form and rank, had pretended to take no interest in the purchase, took her purse out of her sash, handed it to her servant, who opened it, paid the shopman, and then returned the purse to her mistress with the usual civility of first raising it to her forehead. This Daikoku-jimé they hung up in their sitting-room. Then they sent presents, such as large dried carp, tea, eggs, shoes, kerchiefs, fruits, sweets, or toys to various friends and dependants.

On the 1st of January all were early astir, for the father, dressed at dawn in full European evening-dress, as is customary on such occasions, had to pay his respects at the levée of the Emperor. When this duty was over he returned home and received visitors of rank inferior to himself, and later in the day and on the following days he paid visits of New Year greeting to all his friends, taking a present to those to whom he had sent no gift, and sometimes taking his little boy with him. For these visits Yoshsan, in place of his usual flowing silken robe, loose trousers, and sash, wore a funny little knickerbocker suit, felt hat and boots; these latter, though he thought them grand, felt very uncomfortable after his straw sandals, and were more troublesome to take off before stepping on the straw mats, that, being used as chairs as well as carpets, it would be a rudeness to soil. The maids, always kneeling, presented them with tiny cups of tea on oval saucers, which, remaining in the maid's hand, served rather as waiters. Sweetmeats too, usually of a soft sticky nature, but sometimes hard like sugar-plums, and called "fire-sweets," were offered on carved lotus-leaf, or lacquered trays.

For the 2nd of January "Plumblossom" bought some pictures of the "Takara-bune," or ship of riches in which were seated the seven Gods of Wealth. There was Lord Bishamon in his armour; Fukurokujin with his long head and big-lobed ears, who tamed the cranes; the Lady Benten, fairest of goddesses; Lord Jirojin; fat, pleasure-seeking Lord Hotei, and

Lord Ebes with his fish. It has been sung thus about this Ship of Luck:—

Nagaki yo no,	It is a long night,
To no nemuri no.	The gods of luck sleep.
Mina me same.	They all open their eyes.
Nami nori fune no.	They ride in a boat on the waves.
Oto no yoki kana.	The sound is pleasing!

These pictures they each tied on their pillow to bring lucky dreams, and great was the laughter in the morning when they related their dreams. Yoshsan said he had dreamt he had a beautiful portmanteau full of nice foreign things, such as comforters, note-books, pencils, india-rubber, condensed milk, lama, wide-awakes, boots, and brass jewelry, and just as he opened it everything vanished and he found only a torn fan, an odd chopstick, a horse's cast straw shoe, and a live crow.

When at home the children for the first few days of the New Year dressed in their best crape, made up in three silken-wadded layers, with their crest embroidered on the centre of the back and on the sleeves of the quaintly flowered long upper skirt, beneath whose wadded hem peeped the scarlet rolls of the hems of their under-dresses, and then the white-stockinged feet with, passing between the toes, the scarlet thong of the black-lacquered clog. The little girl's sash was of many-flowered brocade with scarlet broidered pouch hanging at her right side, and a scarlet over-sash to keep the large sash-knot in its place. Her hair gay with knot of scarlet crinkled crape, lacquered comb, and hairpin of tiny golden battledoor, with, resting thereon, a shuttlecock of coral, another pin of a tiny red lobster and green pine-sprig made of silk. In her belt was coquettishly stuck the butterfly-broidered case that held her quire of paper pocket-handkerchiefs. The brother's dress was of a simpler style and soberer colouring; his pouch of purple with a dragon worked on it, and the hair of his partly shaven head simply tied into a little gummed tail with white paper string. They spent most of the day playing with their pretty new battledoors, striking with its plain side the airy little shuttlecock whose head is made of a black seed, singing the while a rhyme on the numbers up to ten :—

> Hitogo ni futa-go—mi-watashi yo mé-go,
> Itsu yoni musashi nan no yakushi,
> Kokono-ya ja—to yo.

When tired of this fun they would play with a ball made of paper and wadding evenly wound about with thread or silk of various colours, singing to the throws a song which seems abrupt because some portions have probably fallen into disuse; it runs thus :—

"See opposite,—see Shin-kawa! A very beautiful lady who is one of the daughters of a chief magistrate of Odawara-cho. She was married to a salt-merchant. He was a man fond of display, and he thought how he would dress her this year. He said to the dyer: "Please dye this brocade and the brocade for the middle dress into seven- or eight-fold dresses;" and the dyer said, "I am a dyer, and therefore I will dye and stretch it. What pattern do you wish?" The merchant replied, "The pattern of falling snow and broken twigs, and in the centre the curved bridge of Gojo." Then to fill up the rhyme come the words "Chokin, chokera, kokin kokera," and the tale goes on: "Crossing this bridge the girl was struck here and there and the tea-house girls laughed; put out of countenance by this ridicule she drowned herself in the river Karas, the body sunk, the hair floated. How full of grief the husband's heart, — *now* the ball counts a hundred!"

This they varied with another song:—

> One, two, three, four,
> Grate hard charcoal, shave kiri wood;
> Put in the pocket, the pocket is wet.
> Kiyomadzu, on three yenoki trees
> Were three sparrows, chased by a pigeon.
> The sparrows said, " Chiu, chiŭ,"
> The pigeon said, "Po, po,"—now the
> Ball counts a hundred.

The pocket referred to means the bottom of the long sleeve, which is apt to trail and get wet when a child stoops at play, and Kiyomadzu may mean a famous temple that bears that name. Sometimes they would simply count the turns and make a sort of game of forfeiting and returning the number of rebounds kept up by each. Yoshsan had begun to think battledoor and balls too girlish an amusement and preferred flying his eagle or mask-like kite, or playing at cards, verses, or lotteries. Sometimes he played "Jiu-roku musashi" with his father, in which the board is divided into squares and diagonals, on which move sixteen men held by one player and one large piece held by the second player. The point of the game is either that the holder of the sixteen pieces hedges the large piece so that it can make no move, or that the big piece takes all its adversaries; a take can only be made by the large piece when it finds a piece immediately on each side of it and a blank point beyond. Or he watched a party of several, with the pictured sheet of the game " Sugo-roku " before them, write their names on slips of paper or wood, and throw in turn a die; the slips are placed on the pictures whose numbers correspond with the throw. At the next round, if the number thrown by the particular player is written on the picture, he finds directions as to which picture to move his slip backward or forward to. He may, however, find his throw a blank and have to remain at his place. The winning consists in reaching a certain picture. When tired of these quieter games the "Tori wo oita," a strolling woman player on a guitar-like instrument, would be called in, or a party of Kangura performers afforded pastime by the quaint animal-like movements of the draped figure who wears a huge grotesque scarlet mask on his head, and at times makes this monster appear to stretch out and draw in its neck by an unseen change in position of the mask from the

O'SHOGWATS.

head to the gradually extended and draped hand of the actor. The beat of a drum and the whistle of a bamboo flute formed the accompaniment to the dumb-show acting.

Yoshsan thought the 4th and 5th days of January great fun because they heard loud shoutings; and running in the direction of the sound they would find the men of a fire-brigade who had formed a procession to carry their new paper standard, bamboo ladders, paper lanterns, etc. This procession paused at intervals, when the men steadied the ladder with their long fire-hooks, whilst an agile member of the band mounted the erect ladder and performed gymnastics at the top; his performance concluded, he dismounted, and the march continued, the men as before yelling joyously at the highest pitch of their voices.

After about a week of fun, life at the Yashiki, or villa, gradually resumed its usual course, the father returned to his office, the mother to her domestic employments and the children to school, all having said for that new year their last joy-wishing greeting—

OMÉDETTO.

THE CHRYSANTHEMUM SHOW.

G

THE CHRYSANTHEMUM SHOW.

Yoshisan and his Grandmother go to visit the great temple at Shiba, they walk up its steep stairs, and arrive at the lacquered threshold. Here they place aside their wooden clogs, throw a few coins into a huge box standing on the floor and covered with a wooden grating so constructed as to prevent pilfering hands afterwards removing the coin. Then they pull a thick rope attached to a big brass bell like an exaggerated sheep-bell, hanging from the ceiling, but which gives forth but a feeble tinkling sound. To insure the god's attention this is supplemented with three distinct claps of the hands, which are afterwards clasped in prayer for a short interval; two more claps mark the conclusion; and, resuming their clogs, they clatter down the steep copper-bound temple-steps into the grounds. Here are stalls innumerable of toys, fruit, fish-cakes, birds, tobacco-pipes, ironmongery, and rice, and scattered amidst the stalls are tea-houses, peep-shows, and other places of amusement. Of these the greatest attraction is a newly-opened Chrysanthemum show.

The Chrysanthemums are trained to represent figures. Here a celebrated warrior, Kato Kirjomasa by name, who lived about the year 1600, when the eminent Hashiba Hideyoshi ruled Japan. Near the end of his reign Hashiba Hideyoshi, wishing to invade China, but being himself unable to command the expedition, intrusted the leadership of the fleet and army to Kirjomasa. They embarked, reached Corea, where a fierce battle was fought and victory gained by Kirjomasa. When, however, he returned to Japan, he found Hideyoshi had died, and the expedition was therefore recalled. Tales of the liberality and generosity of the Chief, and how he single-handed had slain a large and wild tiger with the spear that he is represented as holding, led to his being at length addressed as a god. His face is modelled in plaster and painted, and the yellow Chrysanthemum blossoms may be supposed to be gold bosses on the verdant armour.

Next they looked at eccentric varieties of this autumn flower, such as those having the petals longer and more curly than usual; but to show off the flowers every branch was tied to a stick, which caused Yoshsan to think the bushes looked a little stiff and ugly. Near the warrior was a Chrysanthemum-robed lady, Benten, or Benzaiten, standing in a flowery sailing-boat that is supposed to contain a cargo of jewels. Three rabbits further on appeared to be chatting together. Perhaps the best group of all was old Fukurokujin, with white beard and bald head, who conversed with two of the graceful waterfowl so constantly seen in Japanese decorations. He is the god of luck, and has a reputation for liking good cheer, as suggested by a gourd, a usual form of wine-bottle, that is suspended to his cane, whilst another gourd contains homilies. He was said to be so tender-hearted that even timid wild fowl were not afraid of him.

Not the least amusing part of the show was the figure before which Yosh's Grandmother exclaimed, "Why, truly, that is clever! Behold, I pray thee, a barbarian lady, and even her child!" In truth it was an unconscious caricature of Europeans, although the lady's face had not escaped being slightly Japish. The child held a toy, and had a regular shock head of hair. The frizzed hair of many foreign children appear very odd to Yoshsan, who thought their mothers must be very unkind not to take the little "western men" more often to the barber's, when he complacently considered the neatness of his own shaven crown and tidily-clipped and gummed side-locks.

Being tired of standing, the old Grandmother told her grandson they would go and listen to a recital at the story-teller's; so leaving their wooden shoes in a pigeon-hole for that purpose, they joined an attentive throng of some twenty listeners seated on mats in a dimly-lighted room. Yosh could not make out all the tale-teller said, but he liked to watch him toy with his fan as he introduced his listeners to the characters of his story; then the story-teller would hold his fan like a rod of command whilst he kept his audience in rapt attention, then sometimes, amidst the laughter of those present, he would raise his voice to a shrill whine, and would emphasise a joke by a sharp tap on the table with his fan. After they had listened to one tale Yoshsan was sleepy; so they went and bargained with a man outside who had a carriage like a small gig with shafts called a *ginrickisha*, and who ran after them to say he consented to wheel them home the two and a half miles for two-pence farthing.

A TOY FESTIVAL CAR.

THE BABES ON THE SEA.

H

THE BABES ON THE SEA.

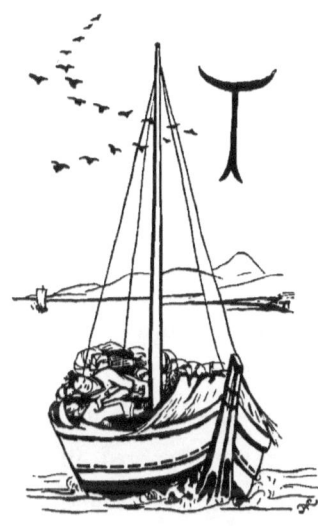

THERE was a certain peasant who lived in the district of Hata in the province of Tosa, and who was in the habit of growing the young rice from the seed in his own district, and then transplanting it, when the planting-out season came, to another province. For this purpose he kept a junk moored in a sheltered creek. Planting-out time having come, the peasant said that now that his little girl and boy had grown quite helpful in the farm they were big enough to go this little sea journey. The delighted children helped to furnish the junk with all necessaries, such as rice and dry fish, and pots and pans, spades, hoes, and grass rain coats, and straw shoes for the workmen. Senzaburo aged eleven, and Yone aged twelve, were then told to take care of the junk whilst their parents walked some miles into the country to hire labourers. The junk was hauled up a little distance on the beach, and the good folks, not doubting its safety, left it there without fastening it in any way. Well! the children fell fast asleep and snored in the hold, and, while they slept, the tide rose round the junk and floated it, after which, as the tide was beginning to ebb again a land breeze sprang up, and what between the tide and the breeze the little craft was borne away to a great distance, which was ever increased by the growing violence of the wind,—so much so, that the junk moved almost as rapidly as if her sail had been set. The children awoke, and saw around them a stretch of sea from which arose none of the points of land with which they were familiar, so that they wept and were wild with grief, and yet could do nothing to help themselves. On they went, blown by the wind, whither they could not tell.

In the meantime, the father and mother had got together their hired labourers and came down to the beach with the intention of getting on board, when, lo, and behold, the junk had disappeared! Thinking at first that the children might have taken it round to some sheltered cove out of reach of the wind, they shouted loudly, "Senzaburo!" "Yone! Yone!" All was silent except the burring hum of busy insect life. Then, filled with alarm, they explored all the neighbouring creeks and beach, but without success, till at last they left off disheartened.

Well, the junk went on, and was at last blown on to the beach of an island far to the south of the children's original home. Still bitterly crying, they made the boat fast, and then looked around them, and found that the island was uninhabited. As there was no possibility of returning home, they went on shore for good, and Senzaburo said, "Here we are, helpless; yet it would be foolish to let ourselves die. So long as the provisions we have with us shall last, we have food enough, and we can eke it out by taking but a little at a time. When our food is at an end, there will be nothing left for us but to die." "No, rather," exclaimed his sister, "before these rice sprouts wither away, let us plant them out." They decided that this was a good idea, and looked about for a place with a running stream, that, by being banked up, could be turned into a rice-field. Having found such a spot they turned to work on it with their spades and hoes, and with the other tools of which the junk was full cut down trees and built themselves a hut. It was the season of berries, and, like little birds, they lived on fruits plucked from the bushes till autumn, when their rice-field, owing probably to the pains they bestowed on it, brought forth most abundantly, and they garnered in a fine harvest year after year until when, long after, discovered by a passing junk, they were able to offer, to their honoured parents now hoary with years and bowed with toil, "Imo-se-jima,—the brother and sister island."

FISHSAVE.

FISHSAVE.

THERE was once upon a time a little baby whose father was Japanese ambassador to the Court of China, and whose mother was a Chinese lady. While this child was still in its infancy the ambassador had to return to Japan; so he said to his wife, "I swear to remember you and to send you letters by the ambassador that shall succeed me, and as for our baby, I will despatch some one to fetch it as soon as it is weaned." Thus saying he departed. Well, embassy after embassy came (and there was generally at least a year between each), but never a letter from the Japanese husband to the Chinese wife, who at last, tired of waiting and of grieving, took her boy by the hand, and sorrowfully leading him to the sea-shore, fastened round his neck a label bearing the words, "The Japanese Ambassador's child," and flung him into the sea in the direction of the Japanese Archipelago, confident that the paternal tie was one which it was not possible to break, and that therefore father and child were sure to meet again.

One day, when the former ambassador, the father, was walking by the beach of Naniwa (where afterwards was built the city of Osaka), he saw something white floating out at sea, looking like a small island. It floated nearer, and he looked more attentively. There was no doubt about its being a child. Quite astonished, he stopped his horse and gazed again; the floating object drew nearer and nearer still, and at last with perfect distinctness could be perceived to be a fair pretty little boy of about four years old impelled onwards by the waves. Still closer inspection showed that the boy rode bravely on the back of an enormous fish. When the strange rider had dismounted on the strand the ambassador ordered his attendants to take the manly little fellow in their arms, when lo and behold! there was a label round his neck, on which was written, "The Japanese Ambassador's child." "Oh, yes," he exclaimed, "it must be my child, and no other, whom its mother, angry at having received no letters from me, must have thrown into the sea, but who, owing to the indissoluble bond tying together parents and children, has reached me safely riding upon a fish's back." The air of the little creature went to his heart, and he took and tended him most lovingly. To the care of the next embassy that went to the court of China he intrusted a letter for his wife, in which he informed her of all the particulars; and she, who had quite believed the child to be dead, rejoiced at its marvellous escape.

The child grew up to be a man, whose handwriting was beautiful. Having been saved by a fish, he was given the name of "Fishsave."

THE FILIAL GIRL OF ECHIGO.

THE FILIAL GIRL OF ECHIGO.

A GIRL once lived in the province of Echigo, daughter of Matsuyama, and who from her earliest years tended her parents with all filial piety. Her mother, when, after a long illness, she lay at the point of death, took out a mirror that she had for many years kept concealed, and giving it to her daughter, spoke thus: "When I have ceased to exist, take this mirror in thy hand night and morning, and, looking at it, fancy that 'tis I thou seest." With these last words she expired, and the girl, full of grief, and faithful to her mother's commands, used to take out the mirror night and morning, and gazing in it, saw therein a face like to the face of her mother. Delighted thereat (for the village was situated in a remote country district among the mountains, and a mirror was a thing the girl had never heard of), she daily worshipped her reflected face, bowing before it till her forehead touched the mat as if this image had been in very truth her mother's own self. Her father one day, astonished to see her thus occupied, inquired the reason, which she directly told him. But he burst out laughing, and exclaimed, "Why! 'tis only thine own face, so like to thy mother's, that is reflected. It is not thy mother's at all!" This revelation distressed the girl. Yet she replied, "Even if the face be not my mother's, it is the face of one who belonged to my mother, and therefore my respectfully saluting it twice every day is the same as respectfully saluting her very self." And so she continued to worship the mirror more and more while tending her father with all filial piety—at least so the story goes, for even to-day, as great poverty and ignorance prevail in some parts of Echigo, the peasantry know as little of mirrors as did this little girl.

THE PARSLEY QUEEN.

K

THE PARSLEY QUEEN.

HOW curious that the daughter of a peasant dwelling in an obscure country village near Aska, in the province of Yamato, should become a Queen. Yet such was the case. Her father died while she was yet in her infancy, and the girl applied herself to the tending of her mother with all filial piety. One day when she had gone out into the fields to gather some parsley, of which her mother was very fond, it chanced that Prince Shotoku Taishi was making a progress to his palace at Ikaruka, and all the inhabitants of the country-side flocked to the road along which the procession was passing, in order to behold the gorgeous spectacle, and to show their respect for the Mikado's son. The filial girl, alone, paying no heed to what was going on around her, continued picking her parsley, and was observed from his carriage by the Prince, who, astonished at the circumstance, sent one of his retainers to inquire into its cause. The girl replied, " My mother bade me pick parsley, and I am following her instructions—that is the reason why I have not turned round to pay my respects to the Prince." The latter being informed of her answer, was filled with admiration at the strictness of her filial piety, and alighting at her mother's cottage on the way back, told her of the occurrence, and placing the girl in the next carriage to his own, took her home with him to the Imperial Palace, and ended by making her his wife, upon which the people, knowing her story, gave her the name of the " Parsley Queen."

A WRESTLER AND A SNAKE.

A WRESTLER AND A SNAKE.

IN the days of yore there was a grand old river flowing by the house of a wrestler called Tsuneyori, and at that spot it was particularly deep, calm, and shaded by many trees.

One summer day Tsuneyori set out for exercise dressed in the thin flax-spun gown *katabira*, with his sash about his waist, and his *ashida*, or clogs, made of a wooden plank with a pair of thin teeth of hard wood, on his feet, his stick in his hand, and a boy attending him by his side. Pausing under the shadow of the trees by the river's margin, to cool himself, he saw that the river flowed past with not a pebble or weed to be seen, only a blue, bottomless depth bordered by rank grasses. He was musing on the breadth of the river, when the water began to move as if something was coming to his side. While trying to make out what it could possibly be, the wave approached him, and a snake popped up its head from the water, seemingly a very large snake. Tsuneyori stood gazing at it, wondering where it would land, while the snake looked intently at him, as he stood about a foot from the water's edge. Then Tsuneyori wondered what the snake was thinking about. The snake after looking at him for some time dropped its head down below the surface, when the disturbed water surged to the opposite side, and after a moment rushed back again. But this time the snake showed its tail instead of its head. Now this tail came nearer and nearer to the wrestler, who remained quite still, thinking the snake had a plan, and that he would not interfere with its intentions. The tail of the snake drew nearer and nearer to Tsuneyori, and at last coiled itself three or four times round his legs. While he was wondering what the snake would do next, it tightened its grip and began to pull. He now understood that the snake wanted to pull him into the water; but, objecting to that part of the plan, he stood firmly, the snake pulling him more and more strongly, so that the teeth of his *ashida* broke, and the situation grew dangerous. Then he exerted additional force and stood firmly, whilst the snake meantime pulled its utmost. By so exerting himself, the legs of Tsuneyori sank half a foot into the ground, and became immovable. Then whilst the fighting-man was in his heart praising the strength of the snake, the brute broke like an over-strained rope into two pieces. The water of the river crimsoned, and Tsuneyori, perceiving the accident, withdrew his legs, the tail following them. Untying this tail, he washed his feet with water, but the rings left on his legs by the grip of the reptile did not disappear. He, remembering having been told that bruises fade away when washed with spirit, went back to his house, and while occupied with his washing, ordered his servants to fetch the tail of the snake out of the river. This they found so extremely large that the diameter of the broken part was about a foot. Tsuneyori also sent his servants to seek for the head part of the snake; and they found this other half, on the opposite side of the river, encircling itself many times round a trunk of a large tree. By this means had the snake pulled so strongly, not knowing, poor thing, that its own body was going to burst asunder.

Tsuneyori afterwards wanted to know the force of the snake compared with that of men. So he prepared a large strong rope, and tied it to one of his legs and ordered at first ten men to draw it at the other end, but he increased the number of men very much, saying continually, "Yet more are wanted"; "The traction is still unequal to the snake's"; "More, yet more." When about sixty men were engaged in pulling the rope, Tsuneyori said that he felt about the same as when pulled by the snake. From this it appears that Tsuneyori was equal to one hundred ordinary men in strength.

A FIRE-CARRIAGE FROM HELL.

A FIRE-CARRIAGE FROM HELL.

MANY years ago there lived a monk in a temple, called Yakushu. Although he was the chief priest of this temple, he never used the funds of the institution selfishly, as he desired after death to enter Paradise. When he got old, and suffered from his last illness, he prayed very much; one day he seemed to be drawing his last breath, but recovering a little, he asked his pupils to come near him, and spoke thus to them:—
"You have seen me ever praying, desiring earnestly to be called to Paradise, but I was surprised to see a carriage of fire leaping towards me instead of a gentle angel. I asked the red, the black, the grey three-toed devil drivers for what guilt I was compelled to go to hell. Bringing the carriage close to me, they replied that I had borrowed a bushel of rice that belonged to

this temple some years ago, and neglecting to return it, the messengers were sent for that offence. I replied that I would return my loan, adding that they might make what use they pleased of my *ten* bushels. Then the devils drove off." After a little while the priest exclaimed, "Now is the messenger from Paradise advancing," and showing his joy by rubbing his hands together, he died. The house of this priest stands to this day on the north side of the temple. If ever such a small quantity of property which belongs to others be used selfishly, the fire-carriage comes to take such an one to hell; what then will be the fate of those monks who spend as luxuriously as they please the revenues of their temples?

THE TWO DAUGHTERS OF OKADA.

THE TWO DAUGHTERS OF OKADA.

AT Akita, in the province of Inaba, lived a *rōnin* called Okada, who had two daughters, by whom he was ministered to with all filial piety. He was fond of shooting with a gun, and thus very often committed the sin (according to the teaching of holy Buddha) of taking life, nor would he ever hearken to the admonitions of his daughters, who, mindful of the future, and aghast at the prospect in store for him in the world to come, frequently endeavoured to convert him. Many were the tears they shed. At last one day after they had pleaded with him more earnestly still than before, the father, touched by their supplications, promised to shoot no more. But, after a while, some of his neighbours having come round to request him to shoot for them two storks, he was easily led to consent by the strength of his natural liking for the sport. Still he would not allow a word to be breathed to his daughters, and slipped out at night, gun in hand, after they were, as he imagined, fast asleep. They, however, had heard everything, and the elder sister said to the younger: " Do what we may, our father will not condescend to follow our words of counsel, and nothing now remains but to bring him to a knowledge of the truth by the sacrifice of one of our own lives. To-night is fortunately moonless; and if I put on white garments and go to the neighbourhood of the bay, he will take me for a stork and shoot me dead. Do you continue to live and tend our father with all the services of filial piety." Thus she spake, her eyes dimmed with the rolling tears. But the younger sister, with many sobs, exclaimed: "For you, my sister, for you is it to receive the inheritance of this house; so do you condescend to be the one to live, and to practice filial devotion to our father, while *I* will offer up my life." Thus did each strive for death; and as the elder one, without more words, seizing a white garment rushed out of the house, the younger one, unwilling to cede to her the place of honour put on a white gown also, followed in her track to the shore of the bay, and there making her way to her among the rushes continued the dispute as to which of the two should be the one to die. Meanwhile the father, peering around him in the darkness, saw something white, and taking it for the storks, aimed at the spot with his gun, and did not miss his shot, for it pierced through the ribs of the elder of the two girls. The younger, helpless in her grief, bent over her sister's body, while the father, not dreaming of what he was about, and astonished to find that his having shot one of the storks did not make the other fly away, discharged another shot at the remaining white figure, and—lamentable to relate,—hit his second daughter as he had the first; she fell pierced through the chest, and was laid on the same grassy pillow as her sister. The father, pleased with his success, came up to the rushes to look for his game. But what! no storks, alas! alas! no, only his two daughters! Filled with consternation, he asked what it all meant; and the girls, breathing with difficulty, told him that their resolve had been to show him the crime of taking life, and thus respectfully to cause him to desist therefrom. They expired before they had time to say more. The father, then filled with sorrow and remorse, took the two corpses home on his back, and, as there was now no help for what was done, he placed them reverently on a wood stack, and there they burnt, making smoke to the blowing wind. From that hour he was a converted man. He built himself a small cell of branches of trees, near the village bridge, and, placing therein the memorial tablets of his two daughters, performed before them the due religious rites, and became the most pious follower of Buddha. Ah! that was filial piety in very truth! a marvel, that these girls should throw away their own lives, so that, by exterminating the evil seed in their father's conduct in this world, they might guard him from its awful fruit in the world to come!

URANAI.
(Second-sight.)

URANAI.

(Second-sight.)

A TRAVELLER arrived at a village, and looking about for an inn, he found one that, although rather shabby, would, he thought, suit him. So he asked whether he could pass the night there, and the mistress said certainly. No one lived at the inn except the mistress, so that the traveller was quite undisturbed.

The next morning, after he had finished breakfast, the traveller went out of the house to make arrangements for continuing his journey, when, to his surprise, his hostess asking him to stop a moment, said that he owed her a thousand pounds, solemnly declaring that he had borrowed that sum from her inn long years ago. The traveller was astonished greatly at this, as it seemed to him a preposterous demand, so fetching his trunk he soon hid himself by drawing a curtain all round him. After thus secluding himself for some time, he called the woman and asked, "Was your father an adept in the art of *Uranai?*" The woman replied, "Yes; my father secluded himself just as you have done." Said the traveller, "Explain fully to me why you say I owe you so large a sum." The mistress then related that when her father was going to die, he bequeathed her all his possessions except his money, saying, that on a certain day, ten years later, a traveller would lodge at her house, and that, as the said traveller owed him a thousand pounds, she could reclaim at that time this sum from his debtor, subsisting in the meanwhile by the gradual sale of her father's goods.

Hitherto, being unable to earn as much money as she spent, she had been disposing of the inherited valuables, but had now exhausted nearly all of them. In the meantime, the predicted date had arrived, and a traveller had lodged at her house, just as her father had foretold, so she concluded he was the man from whom she should recover the thousand pounds.

On hearing this the traveller said that all that the woman had related was perfectly true, and taking her to one side of the room, told her to tap gently with her knuckles all over a wooden pillar. At one part, the pillar gave forth a hollow sound. The traveller said that the money spoken about by the poor woman lay hidden in this part of the pillar, and advising her only to spend it gradually he went on his way.

The father of this woman had been extremely skilful in the art of *Uranai*, and by its means he had discovered that his daughter would pass through ten years of extreme poverty, and that on a certain future day a diviner would come and lodge in the house. The father was also aware that if he bequeathed his daughter his money at once she would spend it extravagantly. Upon consideration therefore he hid the money in the pillar and instructed his daughter as related. In accordance with the father's prophecy, the man came and lodged in the house on the predicted day, and by the art of divination discovered the thousand pounds. Thus *Uranai*, is the art of foreseeing future events very clearly.

NEW YEAR'S DECORATION (page 26).

GAMES.

GAMES.

Some of the games we are daily playing at in our nurseries have been also played at for centuries by Japanese boys and girls, such as blindman's buff,

called *Mekakushi* (eye-hiding), puss in the corner, catching, racing, scrambling, a variety of here we go round the mulberry bush, knuckle-bones, played however with five little stuffed bags instead of sheep bones, which the children cannot get, as sheep are not used by the Japanese. Also performances such as honey-pots, heads in chancery, turning round back to back, or hand to hand, are popular among that long-sleeved, shaven-pated small fry. Still better than snowballing, the lads like to make a snow-man, with a round charcoal ball for each eye, and a streak of charcoal for his mouth. This they call Buddha's squat follower "Daruma," whose legs rotted off through his stillness over his lengthy prayers.

As might be expected, some of the Japanese games differ slightly from ours, or else are altogether peculiar to that country. The facility with which a Japanese child slips its shoes on and off, and the absence on the part of the parents of conventional or health scruples regarding bare feet, lead to a sort of game of ball in which the shoes take the part of the ball, and to hiding pranks with the sandal, something like our hunt the slipper and hide and seek. On the other hand, *Hoi kango*, seen on page 3, is entirely Japanese: in this game, two children carry a bamboo pole on their shoulders, on to which clings a third child, in imitation of a usual mode of travelling in Japan, in which the passenger is seated in a light bamboo palanquin borne on men's shoulders. A miniature festival is thought great fun when a few bits of rough wood mounted on wheels are decorated with cut paper and evergreens, and drawn slowly along amidst the shouts of the exultant contrivers, in mimicry of the real festival cars, as seen on page 47. Games of soldiers are of two types; when copied from the historical fights, one boy, with his kerchief bound round his temples, makes a supposed marvellous and heroic defence, slashing his bamboo sword, as harlequin waves his baton, to deal magical destruction all around on the attacking party; or, when the late insurrection commenced in Satsuma, the Tokio boys, hearing of the campaign on modern tactics, would form attack and defence parties, and a little company armed with bamboo breech-loaders would march to the assault of the roguish battalion lurking round the corner.

Wrestling, again, is popular with children, not so much on account of the actual throwing, as from the love of imitating the curious growling and animal-like springing with which the professional wrestlers encounter one another. Swimming, fishing, and general puddling about are congenial occupation for hot summer days; whilst some with a toy bamboo pump, like a Japanese feeble fire-engine, manage to send a squirt of water at a friend, as the firemen souse their comrades standing on the burning housetops. Itinerant street sellers have, on stalls of a height suited to their little customers, an array of what looks like pickles, but is really bright sea-weed pods that the children buy to make a "clup!" sort of noise with between their lips, so that they go about apparently hiccoughing all day long. The smooth glossy leaves of the camellia, as common as hedge roses are in England, make very fair little trumpets when blown, after having been expertly rolled up, or in spring their fallen blossoms are strung into gay chains.

On a border land between games and sweets are the stalls of the itinerant batter-sellers, whereat the tiny purchaser enjoys the evidently much appreciated privilege of *himself* arranging his little measure of batter in fantastic forms, and frying them upon a hot metal plate. A turtle is a favourite design, as the first blotch of batter makes its body, and six judiciously arranged smaller dabs soon suggest its head, tail and feet.

The games and sports of Japanese children have, however, been so well described by Professor Griffis, that we give as an Appendix his account of their doings.

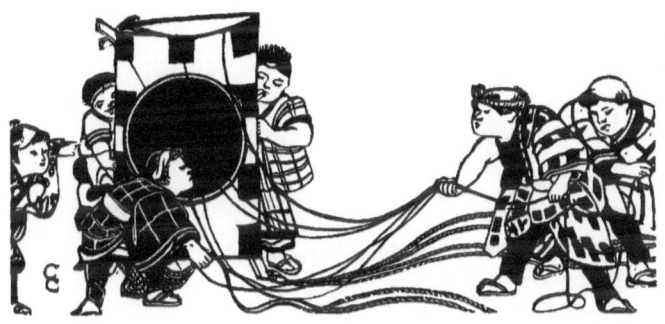

(APPENDIX.)

THE GAMES AND SPORTS OF JAPANESE CHILDREN.

(APPENDIX.)

THE GAMES AND SPORTS OF JAPANESE CHILDREN.

IN Japan one sees that the children of a larger growth enjoy with equal zest games which are the same, or nearly the same, as those of lesser size and fewer years. Certain it is that the adults do all in their power to provide for the children their full quota of play and harmless sports. We frequently see full-grown and able-bodied natives indulging in amusements which the men of the west lay aside with their pinafores, or when their curls are cut. If we, in the conceited pride of our superior civilisation, look down upon this as childish, we must remember that the Celestial, from the pinnacle of his lofty, and to him immeasurably elevated, civilisation, looks down upon our manly sports with contempt, thinking it a condescension even to notice them.

A very noticeable change has passed over the Japanese people since the modern advent of foreigners in respect to their love of amusements. Their sports are by no means as numerous or elaborate as formerly, and they do not enter into them with the enthusiasm that formerly characterised them. The children's festivals and sports are rapidly losing their importance, and some now are rarely seen. Formerly the holidays were almost as numerous as saints' days in the calendar. Apprentice-boys had a liberal quota of holidays stipulated in their indentures; and as the children counted the days before each great holiday on their fingers, we may believe that a great deal of digital arithmetic was being continually done. We do not know of any country in the world in which there are so many toy-shops, or so many fairs for the sale of the things which delight children. Not only are the streets of every city abundantly supplied with shops, filled as full as a Christmas stocking with gaudy toys, but in small towns and villages one or more children's bazaars may be found. The most gorgeous display of all things pleasing to the eye of a Japanese child is found in the courts or streets leading to celebrated temples. On a *matsuri*, or festival day, the toysellers and itinerant showmen throng with their most attractive wares or sights in front of the shrine or temple. On the walls and in conspicuous places near the churches and cathedrals in Europe and America, the visitor is usually regaled with the sight of undertakers' signs and gravediggers' advertisements. How differently the Japanese act in these respects let any one see, by visiting Asakusa, Kanda, Miôjin, or one of the numerous Inari shrines on some great festival day.

We have not space in this paper to name or describe the numerous street shows and showmen who are supposed to be interested mainly in entertaining children; though in reality adults form a part, often the major part, of their audiences. Any one desirous of seeing these in full glory must ramble down Yanagi Cho from Sujikai in Tokio, on some fair day, and especially on a general holiday.

Among the most common are the street theatricals, in which two, three or four trained boys and girls do some very creditable acting, chiefly in comedy. Raree shows, in which the looker-on sees the inside splendours of a daimio's *yashiki*, or the heroic acts of Japanese warriors, or some famous natural scenery, are very common. The showman, as he pulls the wires that change the scenes, entertains the spectators with songs. The outside of his box is usually adorned with pictures of famous actors, nine-tailed foxes, demons of all colours, people committing harakiri or stomach cutting, bloody massacres, or some such staple horror in which the normal Japanese so delights. Story-tellers, posturers, dancers, actors of charades, conjurers, flute-players, song-singers are found on these streets, but those who specially delight the children are the men who, by dint of fingers and breath work a paste made of wheat-gluten, into all sorts of curious and gaily-smeared toys, such as flowers, trees, noblemen, fair ladies, various utensils, the foreigner, the jin-riki-sha, &c. Nearly every itinerant seller of candy, starch-cakes, sugared peas, and sweetened beans has several methods of lottery by which he adds to the attractions on his stall. A disk having a revolving arrow, whirled round by the hand of a child, or a number of strings which are connected with the faces of imps, goddesses, devils or heroes, lends the excitement of chance, and, when a lucky pull or whirl occurs, occasions the subsequent addition to the small fraction of a *sen's* worth to be bought. Men or women itinerate, carrying a small charcoal brazier under a copper griddle, with batter, spoons, cups and *shoyu** sauce to hire out for the price of a *jumon*† each to the little urchins who spend an afternoon of bliss, making their own griddle-cakes and eating them. The seller of sugar-jelly exhibits a devil, taps a drum and dances for the benefit of his baby-customers. The seller of *mochi* does the same, with the addition of gymnastics and skilful tricks with balls of dough. In every Japanese city, there are scores, if not hundreds, of men and women who obtain a livelihood by amusing the children.

Some of the games of Japanese children are of

* The origin of the English soy.
† The tenth part of a *sen* or halfpenny.

a national character, and are indulged in by all classes. Others are purely local or exclusive. Among the former are those which belong to the special days, or *matsuri*, which in the old calendars enjoyed vastly more importance than under the new one. Beginning with the first of the year, there are a number of games and sports peculiar to this time. The girls, dressed in their best robes and girdles, with their faces powdered and their lips painted, until they resemble the peculiar colours seen on a beetle's wings, and their hair arranged in the most attractive coiffure, are out upon the street playing battledore and shuttlecock. They play not only in twos and threes, but also in circles. The shuttlecock is a small seed, often gilded, stuck round with feathers arranged like the petals of a flower. The battledore is a wooden bat; one side of which is of bare wood, while the other has the raised effigy of some popular actor, hero of romance, or singing girl in the most ultra-Japanese style of beauty. The girls evidently highly appreciate this game, as it gives abundant opportunity for the display of personal beauty, figure and dress. Those who fail in the game often have their faces marked with ink, or a circle drawn round their eyes. The boys sing a song that the wind will blow, the girls sing that it may be calm so that their shuttlecocks may fly straight. The little girls at this time play with a ball made of cotton cord, covered elaborately with many strands of bright vari-coloured silk. Inside the house they have games suited not only for the daytime, but for the evenings. Many foreigners have wondered what the Japanese do at night, and how the long winter evenings are spent. On fair, and especially moonlight nights, most of the people are out of doors, and many of the children with them. Markets and fairs are held regularly at night in Tokio, and in other large cities. The foreigner living in a Japanese city, even if he were blind, could tell by stepping out of doors, whether the weather were clear and fine, or disagreeable. On dark and stormy nights, the stillness of a great city like Tokio is unbroken and very impressive; but on a fair and moonlight night the hum and bustle tell one that the people are out in throngs, and make one feel that it *is* a city that he lives in. In most of the castle towns in Japan, it was formerly the custom of the people, especially of the younger, to assemble on moonlight nights in the streets or open spaces near the castle gates, and dance a sort of subdued dance, moving round in circles and clapping their hands. These dances often continued during the entire night, the following day being largely consumed in sleep. In the winter evenings in Japanese households the children amuse themselves with their sports, or are amused by their elders, who tell them entertaining stories. The *samurai* father relates to his son Japanese history and heroic lore, to fire him with enthusiasm and a love of those achievements which every *samurai* youth hopes at some day to perform. Then there are numerous social entertainments, at which the children above a certain age are allowed to be present. But the games relied on as standard means of amusement, and seen especially about New Year, are those of cards. In one of these, a large square sheet of paper is laid on the floor. On this card are the names and pictures of the fifty-three post-stations between Yedo and Kioto.

At the place Kioto are put a few coins, or a pile of cakes, or some such prizes, and the game is played with dice. Each throw advances the player towards the goal, and the one arriving first obtains the prize. At this time of the year also, the games of cards called respectively *Iroha Garuta, Hiyaku Nin Isshiu Garuta, Kokin Garuta, Genji* and *Shi Garuta* are played a great deal. The *Iroha Garuta* are small cards each containing a proverb. The proverb is printed on one card, and the picture illustrating it upon another. Each proverb begins with a certain one of the 50 Japanese letters, *i, ro, ha,* &c., and so through the syllabary. The children range themselves in a circle and the cards are shuffled and dealt. One is appointed to be reader. Looking at his cards he reads the proverb. The player who has the picture corresponding to the proverb calls out, and the match is made. Those who are rid of their cards first, win the game. The one holding the last card is the loser. If he be a boy, he has his face marked curiously with ink. If a girl, she has a paper or wisp of straw stuck in her hair. The *Hiaku Nin Isshiu Garuta* game consists of two hundred cards, on which are inscribed the one hundred stanzas or poems so celebrated and known in every household. A stanza of Japanese poetry usually consists of two parts, a first and second, or upper and lower clause. The manner of playing the game is as follows. The reader reads half the stanza on his card, and the player, having the card on which the other half is written, calls out, and makes a match. Some children become so familiar with these poems that they do not need to hear the entire half of the stanza read, but frequently only the first word.

The *Kokin Garuta*, or the game of Ancient Odes, the *Genji Garuta*, named after the celebrated Genji (Minamoto) family of the middle ages, and the *Shi Garuta* are all card-games of a similar nature, but can be thoroughly enjoyed only by well-educated Chinese scholars, as the references and quotations are written in Chinese and require a good knowledge of the Chinese and Japanese classics to play them well. To boys who are eager to become proficient in Chinese, it often acts as an incentive to be told that they will enjoy these games after certain attainments in scholarship have been made. Having made these attainments they play the game frequently, especially during vacation, to impress on their minds what they have already learned. The same benefit to the memory accrues from the *Iroha* and *Hiakunin Isshin Garuta*.

Two other games are played which may be said to have an educational value. They are the *Chiye no Ita* and the *Chiye no Wa*, or the "Wisdom Boards" and the "Ring of Wisdom." The former consists of a number of flat thin pieces of wood, cut in many geometrical shapes. Certain possible figures are printed on paper as models, and the boy tries to form them out of the pieces given him. In some cases much time and thinking are required to form the figure. The *Chiye no Wa* is a ring-puzzle, made of rings of bamboo or iron, on a bar. Boys having a talent for mathematics, or those who have a natural capacity to distinguish size and form, succeed very well at these games and enjoy them. The game of Checkers is played on a raised stand or table about six inches in height. The number of *go* or checkers, including black and white, is 360. In the *Sho-gi*, or game of Chess, the pieces number 40 in all. Backgammon is also a favourite play, and there are several forms of it. About the time of old style New Year's day, when the winds of February and March are favourable to the sport, kites are flown, and there are few games in which Japanese boys, from the infant on the back to the full-grown and the over-grown boy, take more delight. I have never observed, however, as foreign books so often tell us, old men flying kites and boys merely looking on. The Japanese kites are made of tough paper pasted on a frame of bamboo sticks and are usually of a rectangular shape. Some of them, however, are made to represent children or men, several kinds of birds and animals, fans, &c. On the rectangular kites are pictures of ancient heroes or beautiful women, dragons, horses, monsters of various kinds, or huge Chinese characters. Among the faces most frequently seen on these kites are those of Yoshitsune, Kintaro, Yoritomo, Benke, Daruma, Tomoye and Hangaku. Some of the kites are six feet square. Many of them have a thin tense ribbon of whalebone at the top of the kite which vibrates in the wind, making a loud humming noise. The boys frequently name their kites Genji or Heiki, and each contestant endeavours to destroy that of his rival. For this purpose the string for ten or twenty feet near the kite end is first covered with glue, and then dipped into pounded glass, by which the string becomes covered with tiny blades, each able to cut quickly and deeply. By getting the kite in proper position and suddenly sawing the string of his antagonist, the severed kite falls, to be reclaimed by the victor.

The Japanese tops are of several kinds, some are made of univalve shells, filled with wax. Those intended for contests are made of hard wood, and are iron-clad by having a heavy iron ring round as a sort of tire. The boys wind and throw them in a manner somewhat different from ours. The object of the player is to damage his adversary's top, or to make it cease spinning. The whipping-top is also known and used. Besides the athletic sports of leaping, running, wrestling, slinging, the Japanese boys play at blind-man's buff, hiding-whoop, and with stilts, pop-guns, and blow-guns. On stilts they play various games and run races. In the northern and western coast provinces, where the snow falls to the depth of many feet and remains long on the ground, it forms the material of the children's playthings, and the theatre of many of their sports. Besides sliding on the ice, coasting with sleds, building snow-forts and fighting mimic battles with snow-balls, they make many kinds of images and imitations of what they see and know In America the boy's snow-man is a Paddy with a damaged hat, clay pipe in mouth, and the shillelah in his hand. In Japan the snow-man is an image of Daruma. Daruma was one of the followers of Shaka (Buddha) who, by long meditation in a squatting position, lost his legs from paralysis and sheer decay. The images of Daruma are found by the hundreds in toy-shops, as tobacconists' signs and as the snow-men of the boys. Occasionally the figure of *Geiho*, the sage with a forehead and skull so high that a ladder was required to reach his pate, or huge cats and the peculiar-shaped dogs seen in the toy-shops, take the place of Daruma. Many of the amusements of the children indoors are mere imitations of the serious affairs of adult life. Boys who have been to the theatre come home to imitate the celebrated actors, and to extemporize mimic theatricals for themselves. Feigned sickness and "playing the doctor," imitating with ludicrous exactness the pomp and solemnity of the real man of pills and powders, and the misery of the patient, are the diversions of very young children. Dinners, tea-parties, and even weddings and funerals, are imitated in Japanese children's plays. Among the ghostly games intended to test the courage of, or perhaps to frighten children, are two plays called respectively, *Hiyaku Monogatari* and *Kon-dameshi*, or the "One Hundred Stories" and "Soul-examination." In the former play, a company of boys and girls assemble round the *hibachi*, while they or an adult, an aged person or a servant, usually relate ghost stories, or tales calculated to straighten the hair and make the blood crawl. In a distant dark room, a lamp, (the usual dish of oil,) with a wick of one hundred strands or piths, is set. At the conclusion of each story, the children in turn must go to the dark room and remove a strand of the wick. As the lamp burns down low the room becomes gloomy and dark, and the last boy, it is said, always sees a demon, a huge face, or something terrible. In the *Kon-dameshi*, or "Soul-examination," a number of boys during the day plant some flags in different parts of a graveyard, under a lonely tree, or by a haunted hill-side. At night they meet together, and tell stories about ghosts, goblins, devils, &c., and at the conclusion of each tale, when the imagination is wrought up, the boys one at a time must go out in the dark and bring back the flags, until all are brought in.

On the third day of the third month is held the *Hina Matsuri*. This is the day especially devoted to the girls, and to them it is the greatest day in the year. It has been called in some foreign works on Japan, the "Feast of Dolls." Several days before the *Matsuri*, the shops are gay with the images bought for this occasion, and which are on sale only at this time of year. Every respectable family has a number of these splendidly-dressed images, which are from four inches to a foot in height, and which accumulate from generation to generation. When a daughter is born in the house during the previous year, a pair of *hina* or images are purchased for the little girl, which she plays with until grown up. When she is married her *hina* are taken with her to her husband's house, and she gives them to her children, adding to the stock as her family increases. The images are made of wood or enamelled clay. They represent the mikado and his wife; the *kuge* or old Kioto nobles, their wives and daughters, the court minstrels and various personages in Japanese mythology and history. A great many other toys, representing all the articles in use in a Japanese lady's chamber, the service of the eating table, the utensils of the kitchen, travelling apparatus, &c., some of them very elaborate and costly, are also exhibited and played with on this day. The girls make offerings of *sake* and dried rice, &c., to the effigies of the emperor and empress, and then spend the day with toys, mimicking the whole round of Japanese female life, as that of child, maiden, wife, mother, and grandmother. In some old Japanese families in which I have visited, the display of dolls and images was very large and extremely beautiful.

The greatest day in the year for the boys is on the fifth day of the fifth month. On this day is celebrated what has been called the " Feast of Flags." Previous to the coming of the day the shops display for sale the toys and tokens proper to the occasion. These are all of a kind suited to young Japanese masculinity. They consist of effigies of heroes and warriors, generals and commanders, soldiers on foot and horse, the genii of strength and valour, wrestlers, &c. The toys represent the equipments and regalia of a daimio's procession, all kinds of things used in war, the contents of an arsenal, flags, streamers, banners, &c. A set of these toys is bought for every son born in the family. Hence in old Japanese families the display on the fifth day of the fifth month is extensive and brilliant. Besides the display indoors, on a bamboo pole erected outside is hung, by a string to the top of the pole, a representation of a large fish in paper. The paper being hollow, the breeze easily fills out the body of the fish, which flaps its tail and fins in a natural manner. One may count hundreds of these floating in the air over the city.

The *nobori*, as the paper fish is called, is intended to show that a son has been born during the year, or at least that there are sons in the family. The fish represented is the carp, which is able to swim swiftly against the current and to leap over waterfalls. This act of the carp is a favourite subject with native artists and is also typical of the young man, especially the young *samurai*, mounting over all difficulties to success and quiet prosperity.

One favourite game, which has now gone out of fashion, was that in which the boys formed themselves into a diamio's procession, having forerunners, officers, &c., and imitating as far as possible the pomp and circumstance of the old daimio's train. Another game which was very popular was called the *Genji and Heiki*. These are the names of the celebrated rival clans or families Mainamoto and Taira. The boys of a town, district, or school, ranged themselves into two parties, each with flags. Those of the Heiki were white, those of the Genji red. Sometimes every boy had a flag, and the object of the contest, which was begun at the tap of a drum, was to seize the flags of the enemy. The party securing the greatest number of flags won the victory. In other cases the flags were fastened on the back of each contestant, who was armed with a bamboo for a sword, and who had fastened on a pad over his head a flat round piece of earthenware, so that a party of them looked not unlike the faculty of a college. Often these parties of boys numbered several hundred, and were marshalled in squadrons as in a battle. At a given signal the battle commenced, the object being to break the earthen disc on the head of the enemy. The contest was usually very exciting. Whoever had his earthen disc demolished had to retire from the field. The party having the greatest number of broken discs, indicative of cloven skulls, were declared the losers. This game has been forbidden by the Government as being too severe and cruel. Boys were often injured in it.

There are many other games which we simply mention without describing. There are three games played by the hands, which every observant foreigner long resident in Japan must have seen played, as men and women seem to enjoy them as much as children. One is called *Ishiken*, in which a stone, a pair of scissors, and a wrapping-cloth are represented. The stone signifies the clenched fist, the parted fore and middle fingers the scissors, and the curved fore-finger and thumb the cloth. The scissors can cut the cloth, but not the stone, but the cloth can wrap the stone. The two players sit opposite each other at play, throwing out their hands so as to represent either of the three things, and win, lose, or draw, as the case may be.

In the *Kitsuneken*, the fox, man, and gun are the figures. The gun kills the fox, but the fox deceives the man, and the gun is useless without the man. In the *Osamaken* five or six boys represent the various grades of rank, from the peasant up to the great daimios or shôgun. By superior address and skill in the game the peasant rises to the highest rank, or the man of highest rank is degraded.

From the nature of the Japanese language, in which a single word or sound may have a great many significations, riddles and puns are of extraordinary frequency. I do not know of any published collection of riddles, but every Japanese boy has a good stock of them on hand. There are few Japanese works of light, and perhaps of serious, literature, in which puns do not continually recur. The popular songs and poems are largely plays on words. There are also several puzzles played with sticks, founded upon the shape of certain Chinese characters. As for the short and simple story-books, song-books, nursery-rhymes, lullabys, and what for want of a better name may be styled Mother Goose Literature, they are as plentiful as with us, but they have a very strongly characteristic Japanese flavour both in style and matter.

It is curious that the game of Foot-ball seems to have been confined to the courtiers of the Mikado's court, where there were regular instructors of the game. In the games of "Pussy wants a Corner" and "Prisoner's Base," the *Oni*, or devil, takes the place of Puss or the officer.

I have not mentioned all the games and sports of Japanese children, but enough has been said to show their general character. In general they seem to be natural, sensible, and in every sense beneficial. Their immediate or remote effects, next to that of amusement, are either educational, or hygienic. Some teach history, some geography, some excellent sentiments or good language, inculcate reverence and obedience to the elder brother or sister, to parents or to the emperor, or stimulate the manly virtues of courage and contempt for pain. The study of the subject leads one to respect more highly, rather than otherwise, the Japanese people for being such affectionate fathers and mothers, and for having such natural and docile children. The character of the children's plays and their encouragement by the parents has, I think, much to do with that frankness, affection, and obedience on the side of the children, and that kindness and sympathy on the side of the parents, which are so noticeable in Japan, and which is one of the good points of Japanese life and character.

www.ingramcontent.com/pod-product-compliance
Lightning Source LLC
Chambersburg PA
CBHW030435190426
43202CB00036B/1152